THE ACTION BIBLE

THE BATTLE BEGINS

David ⓒ Cook

transforming lives together

THE BATTLE BEGINS
Published by David C Cook
4050 Lee Vance View
Colorado Springs, CO 80918 U.S.A.

David C Cook Distribution Canada
55 Woodslee Avenue, Paris, Ontario, Canada N3L 3E5

David C Cook U.K., Kingsway Communications
Eastbourne, East Sussex BN23 6NT, England

The graphic circle C logo is a registered trademark of David C Cook.

Narration is taken from the Holy Bible, New International Version®, NIV®. Copyright
© 1973, 2011 by Biblica, Inc.™ Used by permission of Zondervan. All rights reserved
worldwide. www.zondervan.com; and the New Revised Standard Version Bible, copyright
1989, Division of Christian Education of the National Council of the Churches of
Christ in the United States of America. Used by permission. All rights reserved.

LCCN 2014943144
ISBN 978-0-7814-1142-4

Text © 2014 David C Cook
Illustrations © 2014 Sergio Cariello Studio, Inc.
Script by Caleb Seeling

This story was based on Scripture passages including, but not limited to:
Genesis 2:9–16; 3:1–5, 14, Isaiah 14:4–17, Ezekiel 28:11–19, Luke 2,
10:17–18, John 1:1–5, Hebrews 12:22, and Revelation 12:4–17.

The Team: John Blase, Catherine DeVries, Ingrid Beck, Amy
Konyndyk, Caitlyn Carlson, Helen Macdonald, Karen Athen

Cover Design: Rule29 Creative, Inc.
Kirk DouPonce, DogEared Design
Art Director: Amy Konyndyk
Letterer: David Lanphear
Colorist: Patrick Gama

Printed in the United States of America
First Edition 2014

1 2 3 4 5 6 7 8 9 10

080514

ALL THINGS CAME INTO BEING THROUGH HIM, AND WITHOUT HIM NOT ONE THING CAME INTO BEING.

NOW THE EARTH WAS FORMLESS AND EMPTY; DARKNESS WAS OVER THE SURFACE OF THE DEEP ...

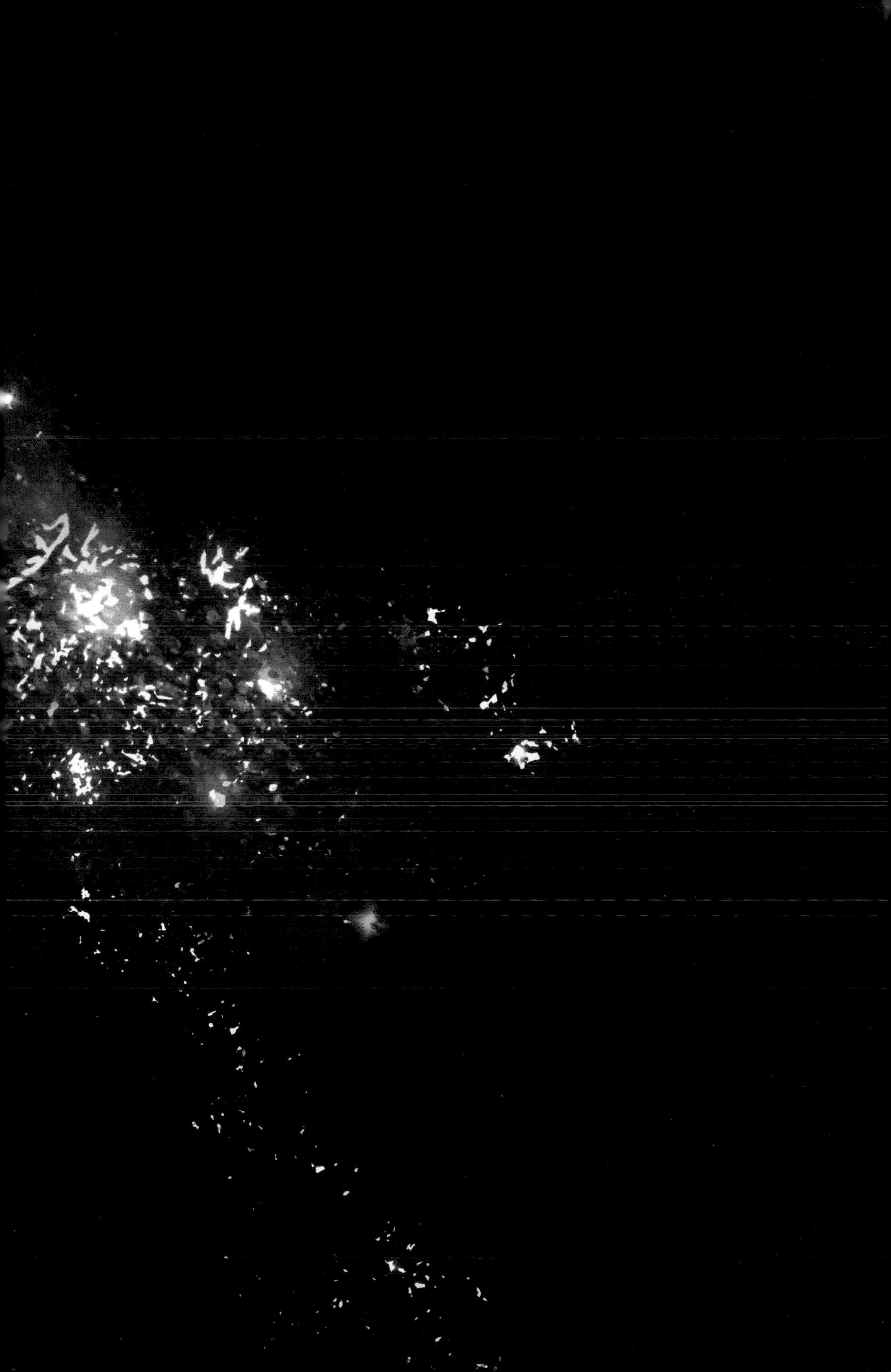

LET THERE BE LIGHTS IN THE VAULT OF THE SKY TO SEPARATE THE DAY FROM THE NIGHT.

LET THE LAND PRODUCE LIVING CREATURES ACCORDING TO THEIR KINDS.

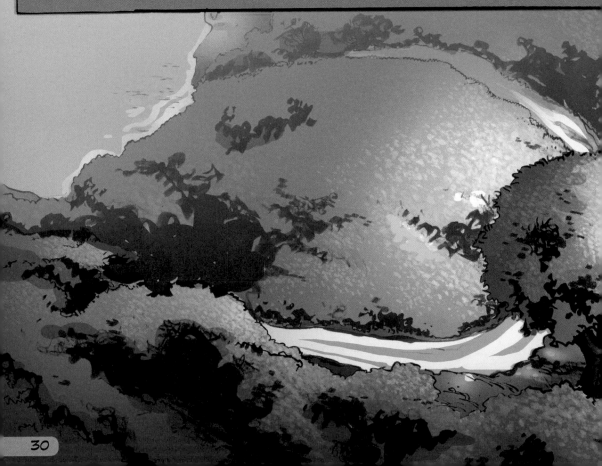

ALL THIS, MY SON... IT'S ALL YOURS.

grROWR

THAT'S A FUNNY SOUND, ISN'T IT?

YOU'LL NEED TO EAT FOOD.

I GIVE YOU EVERY SEED-BEARING PLANT ON THE FACE OF THE EARTH...

...AND EVERY TREE THAT HAS FRUIT WITH SEED IN IT. THEY'RE YOURS TO EAT.

YOU KNOW... FOR FOOD.

YOU'VE BEEN EATING A LOT OF GOOD THINGS, AND YOU ARE FREE TO EAT FROM ANY TREE IN THE GARDEN.

BUT YOU MUST NOT EAT FROM THE TREE OF THE KNOWLEDGE OF GOOD AND EVIL.

BECAUSE WHEN YOU EAT FROM IT, YOU WILL CERTAINLY DIE.

OKAY?

HMM.

GOOD.

NOW, THERE'S A VERY SILLY ANIMAL AROUND HERE I THINK YOU'D LIKE TO SEE.

IT HAS LONG ARMS, SHORT LEGS, AND A HUGE RED BOTTOM!

THERE'S ONE! HAHAHA!

WHAT DO YOU WANT TO CALL IT?

DON'T GET ME WRONG. HIS PLAN IS PERFECT. I MEAN, LOOK AT THIS... WHAT HE JUST DID.

IT'S INCREDIBLE. BUT I WONDER IF HE MIGHT CONSIDER OUR ENHANCED VERSION...

ONE THAT WOULD ALSO SECURE OUR PLACE IN THIS NEW WORLD OF HIS.

I HOPE I'M MISUNDERSTANDING YOU, LUCIFER.

ALL I'M SAYING IS IF THEY CAN MAKE CHOICES AS WE DO, AND IF THEY'LL BE TREATED AS HIS HEIRS, THEN WHY CAN'T WE BE TREATED THE SAME WAY?

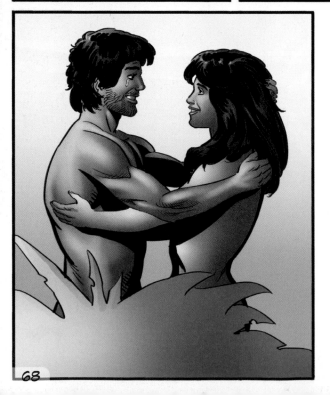

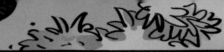

THERE'S SOMETHING I HAVEN'T TOLD YOU YET.

YOU KNOW HOW I'VE BEEN KEEPING US AWAY FROM THIS TREE?

WELL, THERE'S A REASON.

WHAT IS IT?

85

GET OUT.

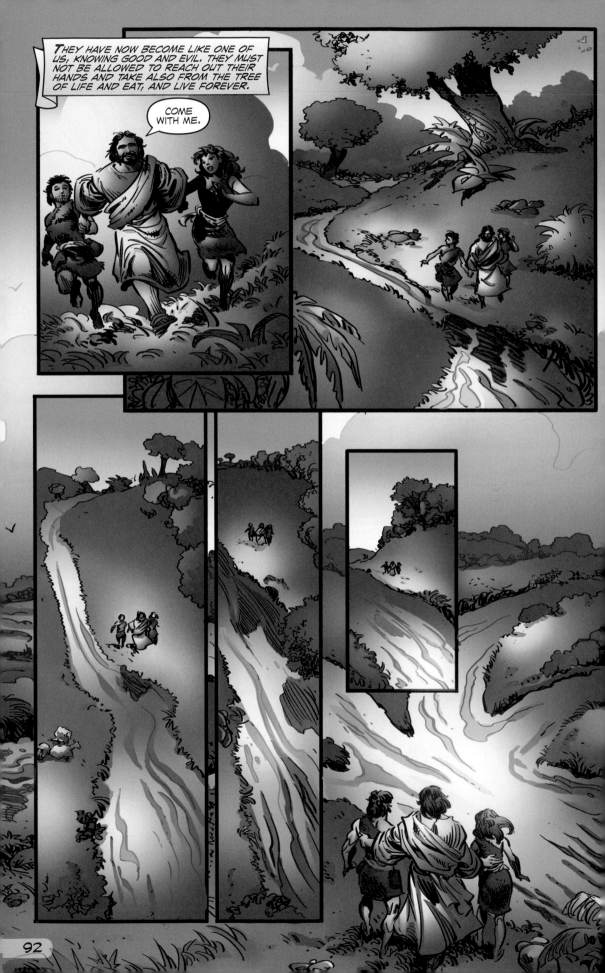

THEY HAVE NOW BECOME LIKE ONE OF US, KNOWING GOOD AND EVIL. THEY MUST NOT BE ALLOWED TO REACH OUT THEIR HANDS AND TAKE ALSO FROM THE TREE OF LIFE AND EAT, AND LIVE FOREVER.

COME WITH ME.

TO BE CONTINUED ...

THE ACTION BIBLE

COLLECTION

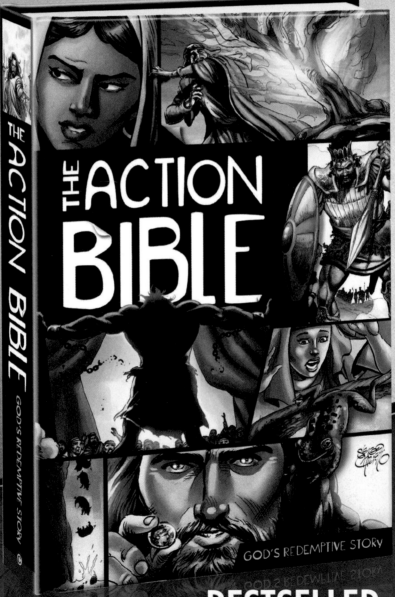

BESTSELLER